The Love Poems of Rumi

The Love Poems of Rumi

edited by

DEEPAK CHOPRA

translated by

DEEPAK CHOPRA

and

FEREYDOUN KIA

Harmony Books NEW YORK

Grateful acknowledgment is made to
Maypop for permission to reprint
the four poems on pages 59–62
from the book *Birdsong*
by Rumi, translated by Coleman Barks (1993).
Copyright © 1993 by Coleman Barks.

Published by Harmony Books, a division of Crown Publishers, Inc.,
201 East 50th Street, New York, New York 10022

HARMONY and colophon are trademarks of Crown Publishers, Inc.

Random House, Inc. New York, Toronto, London, Sydney, Auckland

www.randomhouse.com/

Printed in the United States of America

Library of Congress Cataloging in Publication Data

Jalāl al-Dīn Rūmī, Maulana, 838–
[Selections. English. 1998]
The love poems of Rumi / edited by Deepak Chopra ; translated by
Fereydoun Kia.
I. Kia, Fereydoun, II. Chopra, Deepak. III. Title.
PK6480.E5K54   1998
891'.5511—dc21   97-35690
CIP

ISBN 0-609-60243-8

10 9

❈ CONTENTS ❈

❈ ACKNOWLEDGMENTS ❈

To Rebecca Flynn, Valery Pine-Wright,
and Carolyn Rangel for invaluable editorial
assistance. Your skills truly refined the message
contained in these poems.

To Mallika, Gautama, Sumant, and Rita
for making the message in these poems the
experience of life for me.

To Peter Guzzardi, Chip Gibson, and Alberto Vitale
for helping me bring these poems to the awareness
of the American public.

Deepak Chopra

❈ ACKNOWLEDGMENTS ❈

I am forever grateful to my sister, Vida Belton, who initiated the events which brought me in contact with Deepak Chopra. The resulting friendship and the opportunity for me to contribute to the realization of this book has been a wonderful experience, which has given new meaning to my life. For quite some time, I have been fully absorbed in Rumi's poems and the task of relaying their spiritual message to Deepak, and I wouldn't have felt as comfortable doing so if it hadn't been for the patience and understanding of my family. My wife, Melahat, was not only accepting my absence of mind, but also actively assisting me in the interpretation. My brother Bahman's logistical efforts were most valuable, and finally I wish to express my gratitude to Deepak's team of collaborators, who gave me support and encouragement to an extent which is rarely seen these days.

Rumi's poems are timeless—what he wrote seven centuries ago could have been written today, or might as well have waited another hundred years to be formulated. His words come to us clear and loud, with perfect rhythm and rhyme; simple, everyday words—yet so full of meaning. To fully appreciate his technique and the deeper meaning of his words, it is necessary to have access to the Persian language. But to feel the essence of his message and the moods of his sentiments, it is enough to be human.

Fereydoun Kia

⌖ INTRODUCTION ⌖

In August 1996 I met Fereydoun Kia at a course that I was giving titled "Seduction of Spirit." We are both lovers of the poems of Jalāl al-Dīn Mohammad Balkhi (popularly known as Rumi) and during that week of spiritual rhapsody we spent many moments exulting in the ravishing ecstasy that the passion of Rumi evoked in both of us.

One day Fereydoun introduced us to a Rumi love song that he had translated into English. That evening a woman from the course performed an ecstatic dervish dance while I recited the poem in English, as a friend of ours played music to her movements. Suddenly, the idea was born: "Let's do a new translation of love poems by Rumi that evoke both the agony and ecstasy of yearning."

These poems reflect the deepest longings of the human heart as it searches for the divine. They celebrate love. Each poetic whisper is urgent, expressing the desire that penetrates human relationships and inspires intimacy with the self, silently nurturing an affinity for the Beloved. They are not direct translations, but "moods" that we have captured as certain phrases radiated from the original Farsi, giving life to a new creation but retaining the essence of its source.

Both Fereydoun and I hope that they will give you a glimpse of that beautiful world of love that we experienced as we sought to capture in English the dreams, wishes, hopes, desires, and feelings of a man who continues to amaze, bewilder, confound, and teach one thousand years after he walked on this earth.

The Love Poems of Rumi

The Agony and Ecstasy of Divine Discontent: The Moods of Rumi

• 🕸 •

In the orchard and rose garden
I long to see your face.
In the taste of Sweetness
I long to kiss your lips.
In the shadows of passion
I long for your love.

Oh! Supreme Lover!
Let me leave aside my worries.
The flowers are blooming
with the exultation of your Spirit.

By Allah!
I long to escape the prison of my ego
and lose myself
in the mountains and the desert.

These sad and lonely people tire me.
I long to revel in the drunken frenzy of your love
and feel the strength of Rustam in my hands.

I'm sick of mortal kings.
I long to see your light.
With lamps in hand
the sheikhs and mullahs roam
the dark alleys of these towns
not finding what they seek.

You are the Essence of the Essence,
The intoxication of Love.
I long to sing your praises
but stand mute
with the agony of wishing in my heart.

The Agony of Lovers

The agony of lovers
burns with the fire of passion.
Lovers leave traces of where they've been.
The wailing of broken hearts
is the doorway to God.

The Alchemy of Love

·❦·

You come to us
from another world

From beyond the stars
and void of space.
Transcendent, Pure,
Of unimaginable beauty,
Bringing with you
the essence of love

You transform all
who are touched by you.
Mundane concerns,
troubles, and sorrows
dissolve in your presence,
Bringing joy
to ruler and ruled
To peasant and king

18

You bewilder us
with your grace.
All evils
transform into
goodness.

You are the master alchemist.

You light the fire of love
in earth and sky
in heart and soul
of every being.

Through your loving
existence and nonexistence merge.
All opposites unite.
All that is profane
becomes sacred again.

Aroused Passion

· ·

Oh God
Let all lovers be content
Give them happy endings
Let their lives be celebrations
Let their hearts dance in the fire of your love

My sweetheart
You have aroused my passion
Your touch has filled me with desire
I am no longer separate from you

These are precious moments
I beseech you
Don't let me wait
Let me merge with you

The Awakening

In the early dawn of happiness
you gave me three kisses
so that I would wake up
to this moment of love

I tried to remember in my heart
what I'd dreamt about
during the night
before I became aware
of this morning
of life

I found my dreams
but the moon took me away.
It lifted me up to the firmament
and suspended me there.
I saw how my heart had fallen
on your path
singing a song

Between my love and my heart
things were happening which
slowly, slowly
made me recall everything

You arouse me with your touch
although I can't see your hands.
You have kissed me with tenderness
although I haven't seen your lips.
You are hidden from me

But it is you who keeps me alive

Perhaps the time will come
when you will tire of kisses.
I shall be happy
even for insults from you.
I only ask that you
keep some attention
on me

Behind the Scenes

Is it your face
that adorns this garden?
Is it your fragrance
that intoxicates this garden?
Is it your spirit
that has made this brook
a river of wine?

Hundreds have looked for you
and died searching
in this garden
where you hide behind the scenes.

But this pain is not for those
who come as lovers.
You are easy to find here.
You are in the breeze
and in this river of wine.

My Beloved

·❖·

Know that my beloved is hidden from everyone
Know that she is beyond the belief of all beliefs
Know that in my heart she is as clear as the moon
Know that she is the life in my body and in my soul

Bittersweet

· ·

In my hallucination
I saw my Beloved's flower garden

In my vertigo
In my dizziness
In my drunken haze
whirling and dancing
like a spinning wheel
I saw myself
as the source of existence

I was there in the beginning
and I was the spirit of love

Now I am sober
There is only the hangover
and the memory of love
And only the sorrow

I yearn for happiness
I ask for help
I want mercy

And my love says

Look at me and hear me
because I'm here just for that

I am your moon
and your moonlight too
I am your flower garden
and your water too

I have come all this way
eager for you
without shoes or shawl

I want you to laugh
to kill all your worries
to love you
to nourish you

Oh Sweet Bitterness!
I will soothe you and heal you
I will bring you roses
I too have been covered with thorns

My Burning Heart

My heart is burning with love
All can see this flame
My heart is pulsing with passion
like waves on an ocean

My friends have become strangers
and I'm surrounded by enemies
But I'm free as the wind
no longer hurt by those who reproach me

I'm at home wherever I am
and in the room of lovers
I can see with closed eyes
the beauty that dances

Behind the veils
intoxicated with love
I too dance the rhythm
of this moving world

I have lost my senses
in my world of lovers

Caught in the Fire of Love

· ▨ ·

My heart is on fire!
In my madness
I roam the desert
The flames of my passion
devour the wind and the sky

My cries of longing
My wails of sorrow
are tormenting my soul

You wait
patiently
looking into my intoxicated eyes
You accept my passion
with the serenity of love
You are the master of existence

One day I shall be
a Lover like you

Come to Me

I'm your lover
Come to my side
I will open
the gate to your love

Come settle with me
Let us be neighbors
to the stars

You have been hiding so long
aimlessly drifting
in the sea of my love

Even so
you have always been
connected to me
Concealed, revealed
in the known
in the unmanifest

31

I am Life itself

You have been a prisoner
of a little pond
I am the ocean
and its turbulent flood
Come merge with me
leave this world of ignorance

Be with me
I will open
the gate to your love

Defeated by Love

· 🐚 ·

The sky was lit
by the splendor of the moon
So powerful
I fell to the ground

Your love
has made me sure

I am ready to forsake
this worldly life
and surrender
to the magnificence
of your Being

Desire

I desire you
more than food
or drink

My body
my senses
my mind
hunger for your taste

I can sense your presence
in my heart
although you belong
to all the world

I wait
with silent passion
for one gesture
one glance
from you

Do You Love Me?

· ▩ ·

A lover asked his beloved,
Do you love yourself more
than you love me?

The beloved replied,
I have died to myself
and I live for you.

I've disappeared from myself
and my attributes.
I am present only for you.

I have forgotten all my learnings,
but from knowing you
I have become a scholar.

I have lost all my strength,
but from your power
I am able.

If I love myself
I love you.
If I love you
I love myself.

Dying to Love

Die! Die!
Die in this love!
If you die in this love
your soul will be renewed

Die! Die!
Don't fear the death
of that which is known
If you die to the temporal
you will become timeless

Die! Die!
Cut off those chains
that hold you prisoner
to the world of attachment

Die! Die!
Die to the deathless
and you will be eternal

Die! Die!
and come out of this cloud
When you leave the cloud
you will be the effulgent moon

Die! Die!
Die to the din and the noise
of mundane concerns
In the silence of love
you will find the spark of life

The Hunt

The Lover comes, the Lover comes!
Open the way for Him!

He's looking for a heart,
let's show Him one.

I scream,
"What you came to hunt is me!"

He says laughingly,
"I'm here not to hunt you but to save you."

I Am
and
I Am Not

· 🪷 ·

I'm drenched
in the flood
which has yet to come

I'm tied up
in the prison
which has yet to exist

Not having played
the game of chess
I'm already the checkmate

Not having tasted
a single cup of your wine
I'm already drunk

40

Not having entered
the battlefield
I'm already wounded and slain

I no longer
know the difference
between image and reality

Like the shadow
I am
and
I am not

I Am Yours

Because the idol is your face, I have become an
idolater.

Because the wine is from your cup, I have become a
drunkard.

In the existence of your love, I have become
nonexistent.

This nonexistence linked to you is better than all
existence.

Intoxicated by Love

Because of your love
I have lost my sobriety
I am intoxicated
by the madness of love

In this fog
I have become a stranger to myself
I'm so drunk
I've lost the way to my house

In the garden
I see only your face
From trees and blossoms
I inhale only your fragrance

Drunk with the ecstasy of love
I can no longer tell the difference
between drunkard and drink
Between Lover and Beloved

Looking for Love

A strange passion is moving in my head.
My heart has become a bird
which searches in the sky.
Every part of me goes in different directions.
Is it really so
that the one I love is everywhere?

Looking for Your Face

· ❧ ·

From the beginning of my life
I have been looking for your face
but today I have seen it

Today I have seen
the charm, the beauty,
the unfathomable grace
of the face
that I was looking for

Today I have found you
and those who laughed
and scorned me yesterday
are sorry that they were not looking
as I did

I am bewildered by the magnificence
of your beauty

and wish to see you
with a hundred eyes

My heart has burned with passion
and has searched forever
for this wondrous beauty
that I now behold

I am ashamed
to call this love human
and afraid of God
to call it divine

Your fragrant breath
like the morning breeze
has come to the stillness of the garden
You have breathed new life into me
I have become your sunshine
and also your shadow

46

My soul is screaming in ecstasy
Every fiber of my being
is in love with you

Your effulgence
has lit a fire in my heart
and you have made radiant
for me
the earth and sky

My arrow of love
has arrived at the target
I am in the house of mercy
and my heart
is a place of prayer

Lost in the Wilderness

· ❖ ·

Oh lovers!
Where are you going?
Who are you looking for?
Your Beloved is right here.

She lives in your own neighborhood.
Her face is veiled.
She hides behind screens
calling for you
while you search and lose yourself
in the wilderness and the desert.

Cease looking for flowers!
There blooms a garden in your own home.
While you look for trinkets
the treasure house awaits you in your own being.

There is no need for suffering.
God is here.

The Lover's Passion

· ❖ ·

A lover knows only humility

He has no choice

He steals into your alley at night

He has no choice

He longs to kiss every lock of your hair
Don't fret

He has no choice

In his frenzied love for you
he longs to break
the chains of his imprisonment

He has no choice

The Meaning of Love

Both light and shadow
are the dance of Love.
Love has no cause;
it is the astrolabe of God's secrets.
Lover and Loving are inseparable
and timeless.

Although I may try to describe Love
when I experience it I am speechless.
Although I may try to write about Love
I am rendered helpless;
my pen breaks and the paper slips away
at the ineffable place
where Lover, Loving and Loved are one.

Every moment is made glorious
by the light of Love.

The Mythical Lover

· 🖼 ·

My love for you
has driven me insane

I wander aimlessly
the ruins of my life
my old self a stranger to me

Because of your love
I have broken with my past

My longing for you
keeps me
in this moment
My passion
gives me courage

I look for you
in my innermost being

I used to read
the myths of love
Now I have become
the mythical lover

Precious Love

· ❖ ·

Oh God!
I have discovered love!

How marvelous!
How good!
How beautiful it is!

My body is warm
from the heat
of this love

How secret!
How deep!
How obvious it is!

I offer my salutations
to the stars and the moon
to all my brothers and all my sisters

I offer my salutations
to the spirit of passion
that aroused and excited this universe
and all it contains

I have fallen
unable to rise
What kind of trap is this?
What chains have tied my hands and feet?

It is so strange
and so wonderful
this loving helplessness of mine

Be silent
do not reveal the secret
of my precious love

Surrender

· ▦ ·

In love, nothing is eternal but drinking your wine,
There is no reason for bringing my life to you, other
than losing it.
I said, "I just want to know you and then disappear."
She said, "Knowing me does not mean dying."

The Privileged Lovers

The moon has become a dancer
at this festival of love.
This dance of light,
This sacred blessing,
This divine love,
beckons us
to a world beyond
only lovers can see
with their eyes of fiery passion.

They are the chosen ones
who have surrendered.
Once they were particles of light
now they are the radiant sun.
They have left behind
the world of deceitful games.
They are the privileged lovers
who create a new world
with their eyes of fiery passion.

My inspiration for *The Love Poems of Rumi* was *Birdsong: Fifty-three Short Poems,* translated by Coleman Barks, a book that I highly recommend. There were four poems in particular which I savored in memory, and I reprint them in the following pages with grateful acknowledgment to Maypop publishers and Coleman Barks.

Love is the way messengers
from the mystery tell us things.

Love is the mother.
We are her sons.

She shines inside us,
visible–invisible, as we trust
or lost trust, or feel it start to grow again.

A lightwind coming downhill,
the nightbird's song.

The strange writing I read
on my lover's door

says the same message
now being called out
over the rooftops.

People want you to be happy.
Don't keep serving them your pain!

If you could untie your wings
and free your soul of jealousy,

you and everyone around you
would fly up like doves.

·❖·

In your light I learn how to love.
In your beauty, how to make poems.

You dance inside my chest,
where no one sees you,

but sometimes I do, and that
sight becomes this art.

❈ RECOMMENDED READING ❈

Birdsong: Fifty-three Short Poems, translated by Coleman Barks. Athens, Ga.: Maypop, 1993.

Crazy as We Are: Selected Rubais from Divan-i Kebir, by Mevlana Celaleddin Rumi, introduction and translation by Dr. Nevit O. Ergin. Prescott, Ariz.: Hohm Press, 1992.

The Essential Rumi: Translations by Coleman Barks with John Moyne, A. J. Arberry, Reynold Nicholson. New York: HarperCollins, 1995.

Feeling the Shoulder of the Lion: Poetry and Teaching Stories of Rumi, translated by Coleman Barks. Brattleboro, Vt.: Threshold Books, 1991.

Love Is a Stranger: Selected Lyric Poetry of Jelaluddin Rumi, translated by Kabir Edmund Helminski. Brattleboro, Vt.: Threshold Books, 1993.

Rumi: In the Arms of the Beloved, translations by Jonathan Star. New York: Jeremy P. Tarcher/Putnam, 1997.

Say I Am You: Poetry Interspersed with Stories of Rumi and Shams, translated by John Moyne and Coleman Barks. Athens, Ga.: Maypop, 1994.

The Way of Passion: A Celebration of Rumi, by Andrew Harvey. Berkeley, Calif.: Frog, Ltd., 1994.